The Librarian's Book of Quotes

COMPILED BY TATYANA ECKSTRAND

AMERICAN LIBRARY ASSOCIATION

CHICAGO   2009

Library of Congress Cataloging-in-Publication Data

Eckstrand, Tatyana.
  The librarian's book of quotes / compiled by Tatyana Eckstrand.
     p. cm.
  ISBN 978-0-8389-0988-1 (alk. paper)
  1. Library science—Quotations, maxims, etc. 2. Librarians—Quotations, maxims, etc. 3. Libraries—Quotations, maxims, etc. I. Title.

  PN6084.L52E25 2009
  020—dc22   009000557

Cover illustration ©2007 Oldrich Jelen (www.jeleni.net)

Book design by Karen Sheets de Gracia

ISBN-13: 978-0-8389-0988-1

Printed in the United States of America

13 12 11 10   5 4 3 2

For my mother, the artist,

and my father, the philosopher—

thank you for nurturing my appreciation for beauty and meaning.

Jag älskar dig!

CONTENTS

Introduction *vii*

QUOTES *1*

Biographical Dictionary *107*

Sources *117*

INTRODUCTION

I COULD TASTE THE SWEETNESS OF LIBRARIES from day one. Their wealth of interesting and exciting books instantly appealed to my love of learning and exploring new worlds. When I entered the fourth grade, the school librarian asked if I might be interested in serving as a student helper in our elementary school library. Like a kid in a candy store, I eagerly agreed and was soon spending my extra time shelving books, filing checkout cards, and manning the circulation desk. This new role as a steward taking care of this magical place thrilled me to no end. And thus my career as a librarian was born.

The fulfilling journey that followed—in my many roles as a student library assistant and professional librarian—not only helped to satisfy my constant intellectual thirst for researching and organizing information, but also showed me what an important function libraries play in the education of society. By providing free access to information for all, libraries help to preserve democratic values, and that realization made me very proud to be a librarian.

However, more recently I grew disenchanted with the profession to which I had already given many years of my life. The stress of budget cuts, downsizing, poor salaries, and ever-changing technology forced me to question why I had become a librarian. In hopes of finding comfort as well as an answer to this conundrum, I sought out words of inspiration that might describe libraries and librarians in their true, untarnished light. To my delight, what I found was a treasure trove of quotations and anecdotes that indeed rekindled my love for the profession.

This *Librarian's Book of Quotes* is a selection of approximately two hundred quotes that for me most celebrate librarianship. As you will soon discover, the voices offering us these gems of wit and wisdom are people both famous and not-so-famous, library users and librarians, some contemporary and others long since passed. With sincerity and humor, libraries and librarians are commended from a multitude of perspectives: as champions of democracy, warriors against censorship, preservers of knowledge, navigators of the information landscape, and providers of a welcoming community center and safe haven for the human spirit.

May these words help to inspire all of us who have given ourselves to this noble profession. Or, if nothing else, at least give us a delicious "taste" of it, as in the words of the librarian and bibliographer R. Lee Hadden: "Liberrian: One who picks liberries from wild liberry bushes and makes a liberry pie."

The
Librarian's
Book
of Quotes

COME TAKE CHOICE
OF ALL MY LIBRARY,
AND SO BEGUILE
THY SORROW.

WILLIAM SHAKESPEARE, *TITUS ANDRONICUS*

Th' first thing to have in a libry is a shelf. Fr'm time to time this can be decorated with lithrachure. But th' shelf is th' main thing.

FINLEY PETER DUNNE, *MR. DOOLEY SAYS*

The student has his Rome, his whole glowing Italy, within the four walls of his library. He has in his books the ruins of an antique world and the glories of a modern one.

HENRY WADSWORTH LONGFELLOW,
HYPERION: A ROMANCE

America's libraries are the fruits of a great democracy. They exist because we believe that memory and truth are important. They exist because we believe that information and knowledge are not the exclusive domain of a certain type or class of person but rather the province of all who seek to learn. A democratic society holds these institutions in high regard.

ROBERT S. MARTIN AT A HOUSE SUBCOMMITTEE
HEARING ON EDUCATION

Libraries are as the shrines where all the relics of the ancient saints, full of true virtue, and that without delusion or imposture, are preserved and reposed.

FRANCIS BACON, *THE TVVOO BOOKES OF FRANCIS BACON: OF THE PROFICIENCE AND ADUANCEMENT OF LEARNING, DIUINE AND HUMANE*

The librarian of today, and it will be true still more of the librarians of tomorrow, are not fiery dragons interposed between the people and the books. They are useful public servants, who manage libraries in the interest of the public . . . Many still think that a great reader, or a writer of books, will make an excellent librarian. This is pure fallacy.

SIR WILLIAM OSLER, *LIBRARY ASSOCIATION RECORD* 17 (1917)

A TRULY GREAT LIBRARY CONTAINS SOMETHING IN IT TO OFFEND EVERYONE.

JO GODWIN

Librarians wield unfathomable power. With a flip of the wrist they can hide your dissertation behind piles of old *Field and Stream* magazines. They can find data for your term paper that you never knew existed. They may even point you toward new and appropriate subject headings. People become librarians because they know too much. Their knowledge extends beyond mere categories. They cannot be confined to disciplines. Librarians are all-knowing and all-seeing. They bring order to chaos. They bring wisdom and culture to the masses. They preserve every aspect of human knowledge. Librarians rule . . .

ERICA OLSEN, LIBRARIANAVENGERS.ORG

༄

If librarianship is the connecting of people to ideas — and I believe that is the truest definition of what we do — it is crucial to remember that we must keep and make available, not just good ideas and noble ideas, but bad ideas, silly ideas, and yes, even dangerous and wicked ideas.

GRACEANNE A. DECANDIDO, "TECHNOLOGY IS THE CAMPFIRE AROUND WHICH WE TELL OUR STORIES"

Don't join the book burners.
Don't think you're going to
conceal faults by concealing
evidence that they never existed.
Don't be afraid to go in your
library and read every book.

DWIGHT D. EISENHOWER,
COMMENCEMENT ADDRESS, DARTMOUTH COLLEGE, 1953

My two favorite things in life are libraries and bicycles. They both move people forward without wasting anything. The perfect day: riding a bike to the library.

PETER GOLKIN, AS QUOTED AT WORDSMITH.ORG

A good library is a place, a palace where the lofty spirits of all nations and generations meet.

SAMUEL NIGER, *GEKLIBENE SHRIFTN*

If this nation is to be wise as well as strong, if we are to achieve our destiny, then we need more new ideas for more wise men reading more good books in more public libraries. These libraries should be open to all — except the censor. We must know all the facts and hear all the alternatives and listen to all the criticisms. Let us welcome controversial books and controversial authors. For the Bill of Rights is the guardian of our security as well as our liberty.

JOHN F. KENNEDY, *SATURDAY REVIEW*, 29 OCTOBER 1960

You must live feverishly in a library. Colleges are not going to do you any good unless you are raised and live in a library every day of your life.

RAY BRADBURY, *WRITER'S DIGEST*, FEBRUARY 1976

NUTRIMENTUM SPIRITUS. (FOOD FOR THE SOUL.)

INSCRIPTION ON THE BERLIN ROYAL LIBRARY

A book is a fragile creature, it suffers the wear of time, it fears rodents, the elements and clumsy hands . . . so the librarian protects the books not only against mankind but also against nature and devotes his life to this war with the forces of oblivion.

UMBERTO ECO, *THE NAME OF THE ROSE*

The library connects us with the insight and knowledge, painfully extracted from Nature, of the greatest minds that ever were, with the best teachers, drawn from the entire planet and from all our history, to instruct us without tiring, and to inspire us to make our own contribution to the collective knowledge of the human species. I think the health of our civilization, the depth of our awareness about the underpinnings of our culture and our concern for the future can all be tested by how well we support our libraries.

CARL SAGAN, *COSMOS*

The library is the temple of learning, and learning has liberated more people than all the wars in history.

CARL ROWAN, AS QUOTED IN *AMERICAN LIBRARIES*, FEBRUARY 1995

The library is not a shrine for the worship of books. It is not a temple where literary incense must be burned or where one's devotion to the bound book is expressed in ritual. A library, to modify the famous metaphor of Socrates, should be the delivery room for the birth of ideas—a place where history comes to life.

NORMAN COUSINS, *ALA BULLETIN*, OCTOBER 1954

The richest person in the world—in fact, all the riches in the world—couldn't provide you with anything like the endless, incredible loot available at your local library. You can measure the awareness, the breadth and the wisdom of a civilization, a nation, a people by the priority given to preserving these repositories of all that we are, all that we were, or will be.

MALCOLM FORBES, *FORBES*, 16 FEBRUARY 1981

CURSE AGAINST
BOOK STEALERS

For him that stealeth a Book from this Library, let it change into a serpent in his hand and rend him. Let him be struck with Palsy, and all his Members blasted. Let him languish in Pain crying aloud for Mercy and let there be no surcease to his Agony till he sink in Dissolution. Let Bookworms gnaw his Entrails in token of the Worm that dieth not, and when at last he goeth to his final Punishment, let the flames of Hell consume him for ever and aye.

MONASTERY OF SAN PEDRO, BARCELONA

A library is never—for lovers of the written word—simply a place for conserving or storing books but rather a sort of living creature with a personality and even moods which we should understand and learn to live with.

FRANCISCO MÁRQUEZ VILLANUEVA

The time was when a library was very like a museum and the librarian a mouser in musty books. The time is when the library is a school and the librarian in the highest sense a teacher.

MELVIL DEWEY, *AMERICAN LIBRARY JOURNAL*, SEPTEMBER 1876

Be a little careful of your Library. Do you foresee what you will do with it? Very little to be sure. But the real question is, What it will do with you? You will come here & get books that will open your eyes, & your ears, & your curiosity, & turn you inside out or outside in.

RALPH WALDO EMERSON, *EMERSON IN HIS JOURNALS*

REAL GIFTS

The best things in life are really free
Love, honor, a noble mind . . .
And my local library.

BEVERLY TONA, *BUFFALO NEWS*, 20 SEPTEMBER 2000

No university in the world has ever risen to greatness
without a correspondingly great library . . . When this is no
longer true, then will our civilization have come to an end.

LAWRENCE CLARK POWELL, *AT THE HEART OF THE MATTER*

Even the most misfitting child
Who's chanced upon the library's worth,
Sits with the genius of the Earth
And turns the key to the whole world.

TED HUGHES, "HEAR IT AGAIN"

WE HAVE PRESERVED THE BOOK, AND THE BOOK HAS PRESERVED US.

DAVID BEN-GURION, AS QUOTED IN JOSEPH L. BARRON'S
A TREASURY OF JEWISH QUOTATIONS

Not surprisingly, one good way to start designing an essential school is to plan a library and let its shadow shape the rest.

THEODORE SIZER

[Libraries are] a kind of communism which the least revolutionary among us may be proud to advocate.

JOSEPH CHAMBERLAIN, AS QUOTED IN
JOHN J. OGLE'S *THE FREE LIBRARY*

Shelved around us lie
The mummied authors.

BAYARD TAYLOR, *THE POET'S JOURNAL*

Libraries will get you through times of no money better than money will get you through times of no libraries.

ANNE HERBERT, *THE NEXT WHOLE EARTH CATALOG*

A library is not a luxury but one of the necessities of life.

HENRY WARD BEECHER

There is no better way in this world to lose something forever than to misfile it in a big library.

NORMAN MACLEAN, *YOUNG MEN AND FIRE*

This is a library. Kids and adventurers welcome. All others stay out.

DEAN KOONTZ, *COLD FIRE*

Librarians . . . possess a vast store of politeness. These are people who get asked regularly the dumbest questions on God's green earth. These people tolerate every kind of crank and eccentric and mouth-breather there is.

GARRISON KEILLOR, *A PRAIRIE HOME COMPANION,*
13 DECEMBER 1997

I'VE BEEN DRUNK FOR
ABOUT A WEEK NOW,
AND I THOUGHT IT MIGHT
SOBER ME UP
TO SIT IN A LIBRARY.

F. SCOTT FITZGERALD, *THE GREAT GATSBY*

In the nonstop tsunami of global information, librarians provide us with floaties and teach us how to swim.

LINTON WEEKS, *WASHINGTON POST*, 13 JANUARY 2001

MY EXPERIENCE WITH PUBLIC LIBRARIES IS THAT THE FIRST VOLUME OF THE BOOK I INQUIRE FOR IS OUT, UNLESS I HAPPEN TO WANT THE SECOND, THEN THAT IS OUT.

OLIVER WENDELL HOLMES SR.,
THE POET AT THE BREAKFAST TABLE

A library . . . is . . . a quiet storage place, and what it stores is the memory of the human race. It is a place for the soft rustle of pages and the quiet stir of thoughts over the reading tables.

JOHN CIARDI, SATURDAY REVIEW, 26 AUGUST 1961

SHERA'S TWO LAWS OF CATALOGUING

Law #1: No cataloger will accept the work of any other cataloger.

Law #2: No cataloger will accept his/her own work six months after the cataloging.

JESSE SHERA

Librarians are librarians: they are not caregivers, nurturers, social workers, surrogate parents, welfare agents, or therapists. When all is said and done, their role is straightforward: they gather stuff, impose some order on said stuff, and make the stuff available to the public.

BLAISE CRONIN, *LIBRARY JOURNAL*, 15 MAY 2002

Our libraries are not cloisters for an elite. They are for the people, and if they are not used, the fault belongs to those who do not take advantage of their wealth.

LOUIS L'AMOUR, *EDUCATION OF A WANDERING MAN*

At the moment that we persuade a child, any child, to cross that threshold, that magic threshold into a library, we change their lives forever, for the better.

There are too many books in every public library, and not enough people to dust them.

EVAN ESAR, *20,000 QUIPS AND QUOTES*

THERE ARE ONLY TWO KINDS OF PEOPLE WHO BELIEVE THEMSELVES ABLE TO READ A MARC RECORD WITHOUT REFERRING TO A STACK OF MANUALS: A HANDFUL OF OUR TOP CATALOGERS, AND THOSE ON SERIOUS DRUGS.

ROY TENNANT, *LIBRARY JOURNAL,* 15 OCTOBER 2002

The fact that we as librarians will also tell you what time it is or where the bathroom is does not mean that we're not doing some serious question alchemy to help you find most things. The best reference interactions are ones in which the patrons find what they want and are not even aware that the librarians have been giving them reference interviews the entire time.

JESSAMYN WEST, *COMPUTERS IN LIBRARIES,* OCTOBER 2003

Libraries are the one American institution you shouldn't rip off.

BARBARA KINGSOLVER, *ANIMAL DREAMS*

So the America I loved still exists, if not in the White House or the Supreme Court or the Senate or the House of Representatives or the media. The America I love still exists at the front desks of our public libraries.

KURT VONNEGUT JR., *IN THESE TIMES,* 6 AUGUST 2004

Headnotes arranged vertically make a digest. Headnotes arranged horizontally make a textbook. Textbooks arranged alphabetically make an encyclopedia. Every few years some investigator has to disintegrate one of these works into its constituent atoms, add some more headnotes from recent decisions, stir well, and give us the latest book on the subject. And so law libraries grow.

ZECHARIAH CHAFEE JR., *HARVARD LAW REVIEW* 30, NO. 3 (1917)

When I was just a baby,
before I could speak
I would line up all my letter
blocks alphabetically
and now it's my vocation
and my passion to assign
every decimal-numbered shelf
to every decimal-numbered spine

I'm a librarian, I'm a librarian
and I like it quiet
so the pages can be heard
I'm a librarian, I'm a librarian
and I do it for the love of the word

JONATHAN RUNDMAN, "LIBRARIAN,"
FROM THE ALBUM *PUBLIC LIBRARY*, 2004

One gets thrilled and frightened at the same time in the presence of a library because it reminds one about one's past, present, and, most, of the possibilities of the future.

BILL MOYERS, *WORLD OF IDEAS*

We cannot have good libraries until we first have good librarians—properly educated, professionally recognized, and fairly rewarded.

HERBERT S. WHITE, *LIBRARY JOURNAL*, 15 NOVEMBER 1999

Here, then, is the point at which I see the new mission of the librarian rise up incomparably higher than all those preceding. Up until the present, the librarian has been principally occupied with the book as a thing, as a material object. From now on he must give his attention to the book as a living function. He must become a policeman, master of the raging book.

JOSÉ ORTEGA Y GASSET, ADDRESS, INTERNATIONAL CONGRESS OF BIBLIOGRAPHERS AND LIBRARIANS, 1934

Most of you didn't think that helping people share books would be a subversive act . . . Yet the fact is you have chosen a profession that has become radical.

NAOMI KLEIN, "WHY BEING A LIBRARIAN IS A RADICAL CHOICE"

The categories that a reader brings to a reading, and the categories in which that reading itself is placed—the learned social and political categories, and the physical categories into which a library is divided—constantly modify one another in ways that appear, over the years, more or less arbitrary or more or less imaginative . . . Whatever categories have been chosen, every library tyrannizes the act of reading and forces the reader—the curious reader, the alert reader—to rescue the book from the category to which it has been condemned.

ALBERTO MANGUEL, *A HISTORY OF READING*

The public library is one of the few places left where one can be private.

LAWRENCE CLARK POWELL

The point of a library's existence is not persuasion or evangelism, but knowledge. It is irrelevant to the good library whether, as an institution, it shares or promotes your core values or mine, or the Attorney General's or Saddam Hussein's. The library is always an instrument of choice, and the choice is always yours, not your elected or designated leaders.

ROBERT HUGHES, *AMERICAN LIBRARIES,* AUGUST 2002

Make thy books thy companions.
Let thy cases and shelves be thy
pleasure grounds and gardens.

JUDAH IBN TIBBON, "ETHICAL WILL"

One of the powerful functions of a library—any library—lies in its ability to take us away from worlds that are familiar and comfortable and into ones which we can neither predict nor control, to lead us down new roads whose contours and vistas provide us with new perspectives.

RICHARD F. THOMAS, *HARVARD MAGAZINE,* MAY-JUNE 1997

Libraries and museums are the DNA of our culture.

VARTAN GREGORIAN,
KEYNOTE ADDRESS,
WHITE HOUSE CONFERENCE
ON SCHOOL LIBRARIES

The free library is a living room to an ordinary citizen, a treasury to a researcher, and a chamber of horrors to a dictator.

BENGT HJELMQVIST, AS QUOTED IN FREE LIBRARY OF NEW HOPE, WWW.NHSLIBRARY.ORG

Not only does a library contain "infinite riches in a little room," but we may sit at home and yet be in all quarters of the earth.

JOHN LUBBOCK, *THE PLEASURES OF LIFE*

The free access to information is not a privilege, but a necessity for any free society.

EDWARD ASNER

Show me a computer expert that gives a damn, and I'll show you a librarian.

PATRICIA WILSON BERGER, *CHICAGO TRIBUNE*, 29 JUNE 1990

If truth is beauty, how come no one has their hair done in a library?

JANE WAGNER, LILY QUOTES, WWW.LILYTOMLIN.COM

Librarians: more powerful than a Google search, friendlier than AskJeeves, and the best natural language processor on the market.

ERICA OLSEN, LIBRARIANAVENGERS.ORG

A KEEPER OF BOOKS

I've traveled the world twice over,
Met the famous; saints and sinners,
Poets and artists, kings and queens,
Old stars and hopeful beginners,
I've been where no-one's been before,
Learned secrets from writers and cooks
All with one library ticket
To the wonderful world of books.

SOURCE UNKNOWN

Liberrian: One who picks liberries from wild liberry bushes and makes a liberry pie.

R. LEE HADDEN,
AS QUOTED IN *LIBRARY JUICE*,
12 APRIL 2000

LIBRARY

Here is where people,
One frequently finds,
Lower their voices
And raise their minds.

RICHARD ARMOUR, *LIGHT ARMOUR*

Classification, broadly defined, is the act of organizing the universe of knowledge into some systematic order. It has been considered the most fundamental activity of the human mind.

LOIS MAI CHAN,
CATALOGING AND CLASSIFICATION: AN INTRODUCTION

It takes daily hands-on skill to go hunting for information in just the right way in just the right places. It is a special skill that few home computer users will ever be able to develop to a professional librarian's level of speed and precision.

THEODORE ROSZAK, *THE CULT OF INFORMATION*

For the existence of a library, the fact of its existence, is, in itself and of itself, an assertion—a proposition nailed like Luther's to the door of time.

ARCHIBALD MACLEISH, "THE PREMISE OF MEANING"

Libraries acquire what we cannot afford, retain what we prize and would adore, restore the worn, ignore fashion, and repulse prejudice.

WILLIAM H. GASS, AS QUOTED IN
NSDL WHITEBOARD REPORT, NOVEMBER 2003

They [librarians] are subversive. You think they're just sitting there at the desk, all quiet, and everything. They're like plotting the revolution, man. I wouldn't mess with them. You know, they've had their budgets cut. They're paid nothing. Books are falling apart. The libraries are just like the ass end of everything, right?

MICHAEL MOORE, *BUZZFLASH*, 13 MARCH 2002

A great public library, in its catalogue and its physical disposition of its books on shelves, is the monument of literary genres.

ROBERT MÉLANÇON, *WORLD LITERATURE TODAY*, SPRING 1982

If your library is not "unsafe," it probably isn't doing its job.

JOHN N. BERRY III, *LIBRARY JOURNAL*, 1 OCTOBER 1999

Librarians are almost always very helpful and often almost absurdly knowledgeable. Their skills are probably very underestimated and largely underemployed.

CHARLES MEDAWAR, *THE SOCIAL AUDIT CONSUMER'S HANDBOOK*

As a child, my number-one best friend was the librarian in my grade school. I actually believed that all of those books belonged to her.

ERMA BOMBECK

ANYONE WHO HAS A
LIBRARY AND A GARDEN
WANTS FOR NOTHING.

MARCUS TULLIUS CICERO

Whatever the cost of our libraries, the price is cheap compared to that of an ignorant nation.

WALTER CRONKITE

The library is our house of intellect, our transcendental university, with one exception: no one graduates from a library. No one possibly can, and no one should.

VARTAN GREGORIAN

A library is but the soul's burial-ground. It is the land of shadows.

HENRY WARD BEECHER, *STAR PAPERS*

A library is but the soul's burial-ground. It is the land of shadows.

When you are growing up, there are two institutional places that affect you most powerfully—the church, which belongs to God, and the public library, which belongs to you. The public library is a great equalizer.

KEITH RICHARDS

Few people think about the noble role that librarians play. Our ability to collect, organize, and preserve the voices and observations of those who came before us is critical to our continued survival as a species.

JOSHUA ALLEN,
BETTER LIVING THROUGH SOFTWARE, 4 JANUARY 2003

As a general rule, librarians are a kick in the pants socially, often full of good humor, progressive, and, naturally, well read.

BILL HALL, *AMERICAN LIBRARIES*, JANUARY 2002

The public library has been historically a vital instrument of democracy and opportunity in the United States . . . Our history has been greatly shaped by people who read their way to opportunity and achievements in public libraries.

ARTHUR MEIER SCHLESINGER JR., *LIBRARY NEWS*, WINTER 1982

I THOUGHT I'D BE A LIBRARIAN UNTIL I MET SOME CRAZY ONES.

EDWARD GOREY,
BOSTON GLOBE, 17 DECEMBER 1998

Having fun isn't hard
When you've got a library card.

MARC BROWN, "ARTHUR'S LIBRARY SONG"

The library can become a big factor in raising the level of intelligence in the country and in developing leaders. It can also play a large part in bolstering the faith of individuals who feel frustrated and upset by the tremendous problems that face the world. The more complex the world grows, the more necessary it is to spread the knowledge and wisdom to be found in books.

EDITH PATTERSON MEYER, *MEET THE FUTURE*

I deserve a swift kick in the shorts for all the times I've stubbornly wound my way through the library stacks, my mule head leading the way, searching fruitlessly for information a librarian could put in my hands in a matter of minutes.

MICHAEL PERRY, *HANDBOOK FOR FREELANCE WRITING*

READERS TRANSFORM A LIBRARY FROM A
MAUSOLEUM INTO MANY THEATERS.

MASON COOLEY, *CITY APHORISMS*

One of the great joys of being a librarian is that it is the last refuge of the renaissance person—everything you have ever read or learned or picked up is likely to come in handy.

GRACEANNE A. DECANDIDO,
"TEN GRACES FOR NEW LIBRARIANS"

Death-of-the-library scenarios define libraries as information repositories. If they were no more than that, then their eventual displacement by more convenient electronic repositories would make perfect sense. But the library is a gathering place, too, like an old town square or the corner grocer. People may go to the library looking mainly for information, but they find each other there.

ROBERT D. PUTNAM,
BETTER TOGETHER: RESTORING THE AMERICAN COMMUNITY

To those with ears to hear, libraries are really very noisy places. On their shelves we hear the captured voices of the centuries-old conversation that makes up our civilization, or any civilization.

TIMOTHY S. HEALY, "LIBRARIES AND LEARNING"

In early days, I tried not to give librarians any trouble, which was where I made my primary mistake. Librarians like to be given trouble; they exist for it, they are geared to it. For the location of a mislaid volume, an uncatalogued item, your good librarian has a ferret's nose. Give her a scent and she jumps the leash, her eye bright with battle.

CATHERINE DRINKER BOWEN, *ADVENTURES OF A BIOGRAPHER*

MY LIBRARY WAS DUKEDOM LARGE ENOUGH.

WILLIAM SHAKESPEARE, *THE TEMPEST*

The Internet is marvelous, but to claim, as some now do, that it's making libraries obsolete is as silly as saying shoes have made feet unnecessary.

MARK Y. HERRING, *AMERICAN LIBRARIES,* APRIL 2001

Defend your local library as if your freedom depended on it.

JOHN JAKES

If the College of Letters and Science is the heart of the University, the Library is its soul.

CHARLES E. YOUNG,
AS QUOTED IN *DAILY BRUIN*, 7 DECEMBER 1998

The library is meant to satisfy the curiosity of the curious, provide a place for the lonely where they may enjoy the companionship and warmth of the word. [The library] supplies handbooks for the handy, novels for insomniacs, scholarship for the scholarly, and makes available works of literature to those people they will eventually haunt so successfully.

WILLIAM H. GASS, "IN DEFENSE OF THE BOOK"

After all, if the library truly wanted order it would have one ultimate book on each topic . . . But that is precisely what libraries don't do. Instead, they celebrate the multiplicities of meaning by seeking out dissention and putting it together, inviting the explorer to make their own meaning of it.

BARBARA FISTER,
"LIBRARIES AND THE CARTOGRAPHY OF KNOWLEDGE"

The library is perhaps the best antidote to the insidious influence of the suburban shopping mall. As responsible citizens, we need to give the young a chance to choose between a video arcade and a reading place, a chance to browse in a marketplace of ideas instead of a marketplace of goods and services.

SONNY YAP

Libraries are the key to ensuring that the divide between information rich and poor is kept as narrow as possible.

LYN ALLISON, *INCITE*, OCTOBER 1998

EVERY LIBRARY SHOULD TRY TO BE COMPLETE ON SOMETHING, IF IT WERE ONLY THE HISTORY OF PINHEADS.

OLIVER WENDELL HOLMES SR., *THE POET AT THE BREAKFAST TABLE*

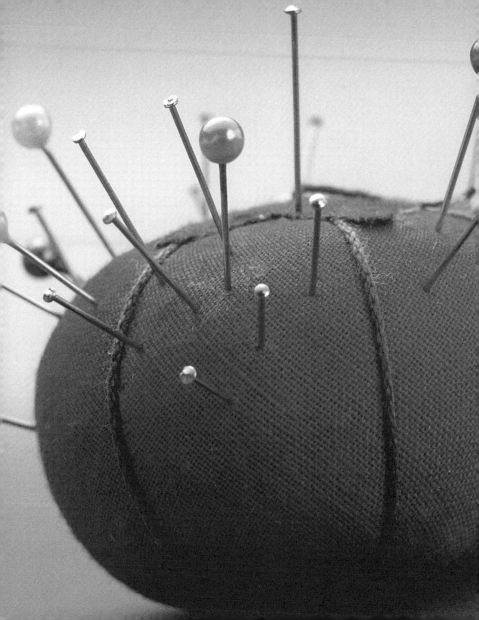

I RANSACK PUBLIC LIBRARIES, AND FIND THEM
FULL OF SUNK TREASURE.

VIRGINIA WOOLF, AS QUOTED IN H. LEE'S *VIRGINIA WOOLF*

**There is a difference between having access to
information and having the savvy it takes to interpret it.**

CLIFFORD STOLL, *HIGH TECH HERETIC*

A library represents the mind of its collector, his
fancies and foibles, his strength and weakness, his
prejudices and preferences. Particularly is this the case
if to the character of a collector he adds — or tries to
add — the qualities of a student who wishes to know
the books and the lives of the men who wrote them.
The friendships of his life, the phases of his growth,
the vagaries of his mind, all are represented.

SIR WILLIAM OSLER, *BIBLIOTHECA OSLERIANA*

Where else could a member of the public linger for over ten hours without being questioned?

BARRY BOWES, "BETWEEN THE STACKS"

LIBRARIES ARE THE CONCERT HALLS
OF THE FINEST VOICES GATHERED
FROM ALL TIMES AND PLACES.

JEAN PAUL RICHTER, *HESPERUS*

I knew I would be a librarian in college as a student assistant at a reference desk, watching those lovely people at work. "I don't think there is such a book," a patron would begin, and then the librarian would hand it to them, that very book. Unromantic? This is a reference librarian's fantasy.

ELIZABETH MCCRACKEN, *THE GIANT'S HOUSE: A ROMANCE*

A library should be like a pair of open arms.

ROGER ROSENBLATT

Access to knowledge is the superb, the supreme act of truly great civilizations. Of all the institutions that purport to do this, free libraries stand virtually alone in accomplishing this mission.

TONI MORRISON, AT THE NEW YORK PUBLIC LIBRARY, 1997

THIS WILL NEVER BE A CIVILIZED COUNTRY UNTIL WE EXPEND MORE MONEY FOR BOOKS THAN WE DO FOR CHEWING GUM.

ELBERT HUBBARD, *THE PHILISTINE*, JUNE 1907

The libraries of America are and must ever remain the home of free, inquiring minds. To them, our citizens — of all ages and races, of all creeds and persuasions — must be able to turn with clear confidence that there they can freely seek the whole truth, unvarnished by fashion and uncompromised by expediency.

DWIGHT D. EISENHOWER, "LETTER TO THE AMERICAN LIBRARY ASSOCIATION'S ANNUAL CONFERENCE"

And the smell of the library was always the same—the musty odour of old clothes mixed with the keener scent of unwashed bodies, creating what the chief librarian had once described as "the steam of the social soup."

PETER ACKROYD, CHATTERTON

LIBRARIES ARE THE "INDEX TO THE WORLD."

JOHN COTTON DANA

Scholars easily forget that they are locked in coevolution with the life-forms that sustain their thought. In particular, they often neglect the evolution of libraries as a vital aspect of their own survival ... in this movement toward collective deliberation, librarians will have to take the lead ... Librarians ... are more likely to see the implications of the coming transformations for the entire educational community ... our coevolutionary fate is in your hands.

TIMOTHY C. WEISKEL,
COLLEGE AND RESEARCH LIBRARIES, NOVEMBER 1986

When life seems not worth living,
ten minutes in the library proves
otherwise.

MIV SCHAAF

A library is that venerable place where men preserve the history of their experience, their tentative experiments, their discoveries, and their plans. . . . In books may be found the recipes for daily living—the prescriptions for the mind and the heart.

GEORGES DUHAMEL, *IN DEFENCE OF LETTERS*

Since my family did not own many books, or have the money for a child to buy them, it was good to know that solely by virtue of my municipal citizenship I had access to any book I wanted from that grandly austere building downtown . . . No less satisfying was the idea of communal ownership, property held in common for the common good. Why I had to care for the books I borrowed, return them unscarred and on time, was because they weren't mine alone, they were everybody's. That idea had as much to do with civilizing me as any I was ever to come upon in the books themselves.

PHILIP ROTH, *NEW YORK TIMES*, 1 MARCH 1969

MY PEN IS MY HARP AND MY LYRE; MY LIBRARY
IS MY GARDEN AND MY ORCHARD.

JUDAH HA-LEVI, AS QUOTED IN RONALD H. ISAACS'S
LIFE'S LITTLE BOOK OF BIG JEWISH ADVICE

So where do you go to find a researcher who is
intelligent, imaginative, skilled in the use of
computers, devoted to discovering the truth, and
knowledgeable about science, technology, history,
and literature, and who usually works for dirt and
gets credit for nothing? After lunch I drove to the city
library . . .

JAMES LEE BURKE, *LAST CAR TO ELYSIAN FIELDS*

Never lend books—nobody ever returns them, the only
books that I have in my library are those which other folks
have lent me.

ANATOLE FRANCE

SOME SPECULATE THAT [CATALOGERS] ARE ALIENS FROM A FARAWAY GALAXY WHO HAVE COME TO EARTH TO TIDY THINGS UP A BIT.

WILL MANLEY, *AMERICAN LIBRARIES*, JULY/AUGUST 1994

NO PLACE AFFORDS A MORE STRIKING
CONVICTION OF THE VANITY OF HUMAN
HOPES THAN A PUBLIC LIBRARY.

SAMUEL JOHNSON, *THE RAMBLER*, 23 MARCH 1751

I always tell people that I became a writer not
because I went to school but because my mother took
me to the library. I wanted to become a writer so I
could see my name in the card catalog.

SANDRA CISNEROS

A LIBRARY IMPLIES AN ACT OF FAITH.

VICTOR HUGO, "JUIN" FROM *L'ANNEE TERRIBLE*

The development of the so-called electronic library in
higher education will impose even greater demands
on academic librarians for, the less visible the
medium, the greater the need for the intermediary.

ALLEN B. VEANER, *COLLEGE AND RESEARCH LIBRARIES*, MAY 1985

The Web is cool, but the library is magic. Where else can the spirit of generations of writers stir your soul? So many writers talk about libraries setting them on their magical paths, it's almost a groaner. But we know it's true. Wander through the stacks and you can feel the dreams, the unique worlds bubbling within each volume. The magic enters you as if by osmosis. On the Web, you may feel clever, lucky and driven to download—but rarely inspired to dream and to write.

ARTHUR PLOTNIK, *THE WRITER MAGAZINE*, NOVEMBER 2003

The library profession is . . . a profession that is informed, illuminated, radiated by a fierce and beautiful love of books. A love so overwhelming that it engulfs community after community and makes the culture of our time distinctive, individual, creative and truly of the spirit.

FRANCES CLARK SAYERS, *SUMMONED BY BOOKS*

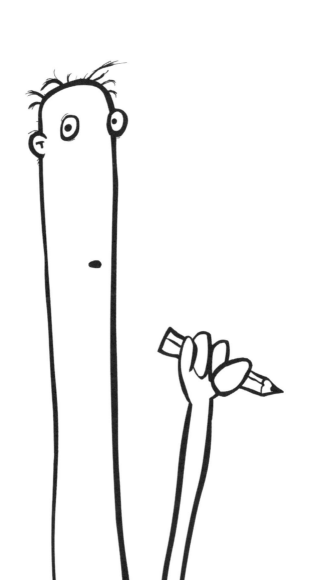

Borrowers of books—those mutilators of collections, spoilers of the symmetry of shelves, and creators of odd volumes.

CHARLES LAMB, *ESSAYS OF ELIA*

The minute I tell anybody that I'm a librarian, they look at me as if I were the last rose of summer . . . I wouldn't ordinarily get so personal about myself, except that I think it's high time somebody made it clear that librarians are people. We do not wear our hair in little buns. Some of us don't even need glasses . . . What I am trying to say is there are married librarians, engaged librarians, librarians who are mothers, even beautiful librarians.

HARRIET FRANK JR., *THE GIRL WITH THE GLOW*

Our library has the most effective search engines yet invented—librarians.

WILLIAM R. BRODY, *JHU GAZETTE*, 6 DECEMBER 2004

A library is an arsenal of liberty.

SOURCE UNKNOWN

The best of my education has come from the public library . . . my tuition fee is a bus fare and once in a while, five cents for an overdue book. You d on't need to know very much to start with, if you know the way to the public library.

LESLEY CONGER

Perhaps no place in any community is so totally democratic as the town library. The only entrance requirement is interest.

LADY BIRD JOHNSON

[The library's] real virtue is . . . it preserves error as well as truth and nonsense as well as sense.

HARRY GOLDEN

[Y]ou do not really leave a library; if you do what it wants you to do, then you are taking it with you.

ELIE WIESEL, AS QUOTED IN *LIBRARY JUICE*, 23 AUGUST 2000

A university is just a group of buildings gathered around a library. The library is the university.

SHELBY FOOTE, *THE CIVIL WAR: A NARRATIVE*

Libraries are like a frosty glass of milk for the American soul—tasty, wholesome, mother-approved and more importantly, a necessary part of a healthy intellectual life.

EDITORIAL, *GEORGETOWN VOICE*, 7 APRIL 2005

If past history was all there was to the game, the richest people would be librarians.

WARREN BUFFETT,
AS QUOTED IN THE *WASHINGTON POST*, 17 APRIL 1988

A good library will never be too neat, or too dusty, because somebody will always be in it, taking books off the shelves and staying up late reading them.

LEMONY SNICKET, *THE ERSATZ ELEVATOR*

The function of a great library is to store obscure books.

NICHOLSON BAKER, *NEW YORKER*, 4 APRIL 1994

The role of a librarian is to make sense of the world of information. If that's not a qualification for superhero-dom, what is?

NANCY PEARL, AS QUOTED IN *SEATTLE TIMES*, 10 JULY 2003

Now, when I read constantly about the way in which library funds are being cut and cut, I can only think that the door is closing and that American society has found one more way to destroy itself.

ISAAC ASIMOV, *I, ASIMOV*

My grandma always said that God made libraries so that people didn't have any excuse to be stupid.

JOAN BAUER, *RULES OF THE ROAD*

The most important asset of any library goes home at night—the library staff.

TIMOTHY S. HEALY, AS QUOTED IN *LIBRARY JOURNAL*, 1 APRIL 2003

A LIBRARY IS THE DOOR TO MANY LIVES.

SHARON CREECH, *NYLA BULLETIN,* OCTOBER/NOVEMBER 2001

Libraries can be an indispensable service in lifting the dead weight of poverty and ignorance.

FRANCIS KEPPEL, ADDRESS, ALA ANNUAL CONFERENCE, 1964

It's funny that we think of libraries as quiet demure places where we are shushed by dusty, bun-balancing, bespectacled women. The truth is libraries are raucous clubhouses for free speech, controversy and community. Librarians have stood up to the Patriot Act, sat down with noisy toddlers and reached out to illiterate adults. Libraries can never be shushed.

PAULA POUNDSTONE, AS QUOTED IN FRIENDS OF LIBRARIES U.S.A., WWW.FOLUSA.ORG

A library is a temple unabridged
   with priceless treasure.
Librarians are the majesties who
   loan the jewels of measure.
They welcome to the kingdom the
   young and old of reapers
and reign among the riches as the
   wondrous keystone keepers.

PAM MUÑOZ RYAN, AASL CONFERENCE, 2003

Our whole American way of life is a great war of ideas, and librarians are the arms dealers selling weapons to both sides.

JAMES QUINN, 1990 WESTPAC/NOCALL JOINT MEETING

From his refined accent, quiet voice and apparent omniscience, I took him for a librarian.

GEORGE ORWELL, *THE ROAD TO WIGAN PIER DIARY*

WITHOUT LIBRARIES WHAT HAVE WE?
WE HAVE NO PAST AND NO FUTURE.

RAY BRADBURY

Reference librarians are a library's eyes and ears.

CHARLES W. BAILEY JR., "THE ROLE OF REFERENCE LIBRARIANS
IN INSTITUTIONAL REPOSITORIES"

We know that without libraries, without education, which is based largely on libraries, we cannot have an educated people who will carry on successfully our form of government.

ELEANOR ROOSEVELT, "WHAT LIBRARIES MEAN TO THE NATION"

A good librarian knows that the best way to file a book is to understand how a reader would classify it themselves.

ROGER WARNER, "LIBRARIANS ARE THE NEW NAPOLEONS"

Believers and doers are what we need — faithful librarians who are humble in the presence of books . . . To be in a library is one of the purest of all experiences. This awareness of a library's unique, even sacred nature, is what should be instilled in our neophytes.

LAWRENCE CLARK POWELL, *A PASSION FOR BOOKS*

I think we need public libraries in the same way we need wilderness. Both are sanctuaries of a king. Both are storehouses of diversity.

ANNA KIRKPATRICK, "ROUNDING OUT THE SUMMER"

Book lovers will understand me, and they will know
too, that part of the pleasure of a library lies in its very
existence.

JAN MORRIS

He that revels in a well-chosen library has innumerable
dishes, all of admirable flavour.

WILLIAM GODWIN, *THE ENQUIRER*

If we didn't have libraries, many people thirsty for
knowledge would dehydrate.

MEGAN JO TETRICK

Existing libraries, in their very being, seem to question
the authority of those in power.

ALBERTO MANGUEL, *INDEX ON CENSORSHIP*, MARCH 1999

Libraries are the wardrobes of literature; whence men properly informed may bring forth something for ornament, much for curiosity, and more for use.

GEORGE DYER,
HISTORY OF THE UNIVERSITY AND COLLEGES OF CAMBRIDGE

The impious maintain that nonsense is normal in the Library and that reasonable (or even humble and pure coherence) is a miraculous exception.

JORGE LUIS BORGES, *THE LIBRARY OF BABEL*

Were this library built and the fond mother would say, "Where is my boy tonight?" and the response should be, "He is at the Library," she could thank God that he is where no harm would come him.

D. C. SWAN WINTERSMITH

To my thinking, a great librarian must have a clear head, a strong hand, and above all, a great heart ... and I am inclined to think that most of the men who achieve this greatness will be women.

MELVIL DEWEY, *LIBRARY JOURNAL*, JANUARY 1899

Librarianship has for its purpose the maintenance of the part of the life of the individual which is the activity of thinking freely.

A. BROADFIELD, *A PHILOSOPHY OF LIBRARIANSHIP*

For those without money, the road to the treasure house of the imagination begins at the public library.

PETE HAMILL, *NEW YORK DAILY NEWS*, 25 FEBRUARY 2002

. . . that perfect tranquility of life, which is nowhere to be found but in retreat, a faithful friend, and a good library.

APHRA BEHN, *THE LUCKY MISTAKE*

When I step into this library, I cannot understand why I ever step out of it.

MARIE DE SÉVIGNÉ, *LETTERS OF MADAME DE SÉVIGNÉ TO HER DAUGHTER AND HER FRIENDS*

There is not such a cradle of democracy upon the earth as the Free Public Library, this republic of letters, where neither rank, office, nor wealth receives the slightest consideration.

ANDREW CARNEGIE

A public library is the most enduring of memorials, the trustiest monument for the presentation of an event or a name or an affection; for it, and it only, is respected by wars and revolutions, and survives them.

MARK TWAIN, "LETTER TO THE MILLICENT LIBRARY,"
22 FEBRUARY 1894

THE LOVE OF LEARNING,
THE SEQUESTERED NOOKS,
AND ALL THE SWEET SERENITY OF BOOKS.

HENRY WADSWORTH LONGFELLOW, "MORITURI SALUTAMUS"

I must say that I find television very educational. The minute somebody turns it on, I go to the library and read a book.

GROUCHO MARX

Of all the professions, librarianship is probably the most derivative and synthetic, and is the most dependent upon the more formal disciplines for its own theoretical structure and its corpus of practice. In the past librarians have been disposed to view this characteristic as a fundamental weakness, and it has therefore generated a considerable feeling of professional inferiority. Yet this very quality has given librarianship a uniquely strategic position of leadership in the integration of human knowledge, and it could make of librarianship a great unifying force, not only in the world of scholarship, but also throughout all human life.

JESSE SHERA,
THE FOUNDATIONS FOR EDUCATION IN LIBRARIANSHIP

Librarians see themselves as the guardians of the First Amendment. You got a thousand Mother Joneses at the barricades! I love the librarians, and I am grateful for them!

MICHAEL MOORE, SALON, 7 JANUARY 2002

I'm not comfortable being preachy, but more people need to start spending as much time in the library as they do on the basketball court.

KAREEM ABDUL-JABBAR

When the lights go out in our libraries, the Dark Ages are coming again!

MITCH HAGER, AS QUOTED IN G. EDWARD NICHOLS'S
THE NORMAN WILLIAMS PUBLIC LIBRARY

There was one place where I could find out who I was and what I was going to become. And that was the Public Library.

JERZY KOSINSKI,
TESTIMONIAL FOR THE NEW YORK PUBLIC LIBRARY

Libraries are fun, educational, and the biggest bargain on the face of the earth.

MADELINE ALBRIGHT,
KEYNOTE ADDRESS, ALA ANNUAL CONFERENCE, 2006

I have never met a public librarian who approved of censorship or one who failed to practice it in some measure.

LEON CARNOVSKY, *LIBRARY QUARTERLY* 20 (1950)

To furnish the means of acquiring knowledge is the greatest benefit that can be conferred upon mankind. It prolongs life itself and enlarges the sphere of existence.

JOHN QUINCY ADAMS,
NATIONAL INTELLIGENCER, 17 FEBRUARY 1836

To me, nothing can be more important than giving children books. It's better to be giving books to children than drug treatment to them when they're 15 years old. Did it ever occur to anyone that if you put nice libraries in public schools you wouldn't have to put them in prisons?

FRAN LEBOWITZ,
AS QUOTED IN THE *NEW YORK TIMES,* 10 AUGUST 1994

234

HUTTON, S - HYPERTENSIVE D

I mourn the loss of the old card catalogs, not because I'm a luddite, but because the oaken trays of yesteryear offered the researcher an element of random utility and felicitous surprise through encounters with adjacent cards, information by chance that is different in kind from the computer's ramified but rigid order.

ANNIE PROULX, "ON THE ROAD TO PROSE"

I pray that no child of mine would ever descend into such a place as a library. They are indeed most dangerous places and unfortunate is she or he who is lured into such a hellhole of enjoyment, stimulus, facts, passion and fun.

WILLY RUSSELL

The three most important documents a free society gives are a birth certificate, a passport, and a library card.

E. L. DOCTOROW, *NEW YORK TIMES*, 27 MARCH 1994

What a place to be in is an old library! It seems as though all the souls of all the writers that have bequeathed their labours to these Bodleians were reposing here as in some dormitory, or middle state. I do not want to handle, to profane the leaves, their winding-sheets. I could as soon dislodge a shade. I seem to inhale learning, walking amid their foliage; and the odor of their old moth-scented coverings is fragrant as the first bloom of the sciential apples which grew amid the happy orchard.

CHARLES LAMB, *ESSAYS OF ELIA*

Libraries give students and faculties a contact with the great minds of the past, a contact that is at the heart of all learning.

JOHN P. RAYNOR

There it is: that wonderful library smell. How could I have forgotten it? The feel of libraries—the way they look, smell, sound—lingers intensely as the memories of a fierce first love.

SUSAN ALLEN TOTH, *READING ROOMS*

Librarians don't have a lot of status, and we don't make a lot of money, more than poets, but not so much, say, as your more successful panhandlers, so our ideals are important to us and the love of books and the love of knowledge and the love of truth and free information and letting people discover things for themselves . . .

LARRY BEINHART, *THE LIBRARIAN*

As the strata of the earth preserve in succession the living creatures of past epochs, so the shelves of libraries preserve in succession the errors of the past and their expectations, which like the former were very lively and made a great commotion in their own age but now stand petrified and stiff in place where only the literary paleontologist regards them.

ARTHUR SCHOPENHAUER, *ESSAYS AND APHORISMS*

HE IS WISE WHO KNOWS THE SOURCES
OF KNOWLEDGE—WHERE IT IS WRITTEN
AND WHERE IT IS TO BE FOUND.

A. A. HODGE

Blaming the library for exposure to pornography is like blaming the lake if your child walks up to it alone, falls in and then drowns.

DAVID SAWYER, *SPOKESMAN-REVIEW*, 18 DECEMBER 2000

The library is not only there as a socially owned and governed institution, a true people's information service; it is staffed by men and women who maintain high respect for intellectual values. Because they are also the traditional keepers of the books, the librarians have a healthy sense of the hierarchical relationship between data and ideas, facts and knowledge.

THEODORE ROSZAK, *THE CULT OF INFORMATION*

Librarians are from Venus; Technologists are from Mars.

DOUG JOHNSON, *TECHNOLOGY CONNECTION*, MAY-JUNE 1998

A library doesn't need windows. A library is a window.

STEWART BRAND, *HOW BUILDINGS LEARN*

THOU CAN'ST NOT DIE.
HERE THOU ART MORE THAN SAFE
WHERE EVERY BOOK IS THY EPITAPH.

HENRY VAUGHAN, "ON SIR THOMAS BODLEY'S LIBRARY"

The closest we will ever come to an orderly universe is a good library.

ASHLEIGH BRILLIANT, *POT-SHOTS*

Information is a basic human right and the fundamental foundation for the formation of democratic institutions.

NELSON MANDELA

My childhood library was small enough not to be intimidating. And yet I felt the whole world was contained in those two rooms. I could walk any aisle and smell wisdom.

RITA DOVE

The death of a library, any library, suggests that the community has lost its soul.

KURT VONNEGUT JR., *HARTFORD COURANT,* 31 JANUARY 1995

It seems to me that libraries stand, above all, for the enlightened and rational notion that human beings are improved by the acquisition of knowledge and information and that no bar should be placed in their way.

MICHAEL GORMAN, "THE VALUE AND VALUES OF LIBRARIES"

Libraries store the energy that fuels the imagination. They open up windows to the world and inspire us to explore and achieve, and contribute to improving our quality of life. Libraries change lives for the better.

SIDNEY SHELDON

A GREAT LIBRARY CONTAINS THE DIARY OF THE HUMAN RACE.

GEORGE MERCER DAWSON, ADDRESS,
OPENING OF THE BIRMINGHAM FREE LIBRARY, 26 OCTOBER 1866

Librarians are not just gatekeepers to knowledge, they are what the American Indians used to call their special sages who preserved the oral legends of a tribe: dreamkeepers.

JAMES H. BILLINGTON,
ADDRESS, ALA ANNUAL CONFERENCE, 1999

I HAVE ALWAYS IMAGINED THAT PARADISE WILL BE SOME KIND OF LIBRARY.

JORGE LUIS BORGES, "POEM OF THE GIFTS"

BIOGRAPHICAL DICTIONARY

ABDUL-JABBAR, KAREEM (1947–) American professional basketball player

ACKROYD, PETER (1949–) English author

ADAMS, JOHN QUINCY (1767–1848) Sixth president of the United States

ALBRIGHT, MADELINE (1937–) American professor and U.S. Secretary of State

ALLEN, JOSHUA American program manager and software blogger

ALLISON, LYN (1946–) Australian politician and senator

ARMOUR, RICHARD (1906–1989) American poet and author

ASIMOV, ISAAC (1920–1992) Russian-born American author and professor

ASNER, EDWARD (1929–) American actor

BACON , FRANCIS (1561–1626) English philosopher, statesman, and author

BAILEY, CHARLES W., JR. (1950–) American librarian and author

BAKER, NICHOLSON (1957–) American author

BAUER, JOAN (1951–) American author of young adult literature

BEECHER, HENRY WARD (1813–1887) American abolitionist, social reformer, and Congregationalist clergyman

BEHN, APHRA (1640–1689) English author and dramatist

BEINHART, LARRY American author

BEN-GURION, DAVID (1886–1973) First prime minister of Israel

BERGER, PATRICIA WILSON American librarian and 1989–90 president of the American Library Association

BERRY, JOHN N., III (1933–) American editor of *Library Journal*

BILLINGTON, JAMES H. (1929–) American author, professor, and Librarian of Congress

BOMBECK, ERMA (1927–1996) American humorist and columnist

BORGES, JORGE LUIS (1899–1986) Argentine author

BOWEN, CATHERINE DRINKER (1897–1973) American biographer

BOWES, BARRY English author

BRADBURY, RAY (1920–) American science fiction writer

BRAND, STEWART (1938–) American author, editor, and creator of *The Whole Earth Catalog*

BRILLIANT, ASHLEIGH (1933–) English-born author and cartoonist

BROADFIELD, A. British librarian and author

BRODY, WILLIAM R. (1944–) American professor of radiology and engineering and president of Johns Hopkins University

BROWN, MARC (1946–) American children's book author

BUFFETT, WARREN (1930–) American investor, businessman, and philanthropist

BURKE, JAMES LEE (1936–) American mystery writer

CARNEGIE, ANDREW (1835–1919) Scottish-born industrialist, businessman, and philanthropist

CARNOVSKY, LEON (1903–1975) American librarian, editor, and professor

CHAMBERLAIN, JOSEPH (1836–1914) British politician, businessman, and statesman

CHAFEE, ZECHARIAH, JR. (1885–1957) American legal scholar, philosopher, and civil libertarian

CHAN, LOIS MAI (1934–) American author and professor of library science

CIARDI, JOHN (1916–1986) American poet, translator, and etymologist

CICERO, MARCUS TULLIUS (106 BC–43 BC) Roman statesman, lawyer, and philosopher

CISNEROS, SANDRA (1954–) American novelist, poet, and short story writer

COOLEY, MASON (1927–2002) American aphorist and professor of English

CONGER, LESLEY American writer

COUSINS, NORMAN (1915–1990) American political journalist, professor, and world peace advocate

CREECH, SHARON (1945–) American children's book author

CRONIN, BLAISE (1949–) Irish author, editor, and professor of information science

CRONKITE, WALTER (1916–) American broadcast journalist

DANA, JOHN COTTON (1856–1929) American librarian and museum director

DAWSON, GEORGE MERCER (1849–1901) Canadian scientist and surveyor

DECANDIDO, GRACEANNE A. American writer, teacher, and librarian

DEWEY, MELVIL (1851–1931) American librarian and inventor of the Dewey Decimal Classification system

DOCTOROW, E. L. (1931–) American author

DOVE, RITA (1952–) Pulitzer Prize–winning American poet and author

DUHAMEL, GEORGES (1884–1966) French author

DUNNE, FINLEY PETER (1867–1936) American journalist and humorist

DYER, GEORGE (1755–1841) English classicist and author

ECO, UMBERTO (1932–) Italian medievalist, novelist, and philosopher

EISENHOWER, DWIGHT D. (1890–1969) General of the U.S. Army and thirty-fourth president of the United States

EMERSON, RALPH WALDO (1803–1882) American essayist, philosopher, poet, and leader of the Transcendentalist movement

ESAR, EVAN (1899–1995) American humorist

FISTER, BARBARA American librarian and author

FITZGERALD, F. SCOTT (1896–1940) American novelist and short story writer

FOOTE, SHELBY (1916–2005) American novelist and Civil War historian

FORBES, MALCOLM (1919–1990) American publisher of *Forbes* magazine

FRANCE, ANATOLE (1844–1924) Nobel Prize–winning French poet, journalist, and novelist

FRANK, HARRIET, JR. (1917–) American screenwriter and producer

GASS, WILLIAM H. (1924–) American novelist, short story writer, critic, and philosophy professor

GODWIN, WILLIAM (1756–1836) English journalist, political philosopher, and novelist

GOLDEN, HARRY (1902–1981) American Jewish writer and newspaper publisher

GOLKIN, PETER (1966–) U.S. museum spokesperson

GOREY, EDWARD (1925–2000) American writer and artist

GORMAN, MICHAEL (1941–) English-born American librarian and author

GREGORIAN, VARTAN (1934–) American academic and president of the Carnegie Corporation of New York

HADDEN, R. LEE (1951–) American librarian

HALL, BILL (1937–) American humorist, editor, and writer

HAMILL, PETE (1935–) American journalist, essayist, and novelist

HEALY, TIMOTHY S. (1923–1992) Jesuit priest and president of both Georgetown University and New York Public Library

HERBERT, ANNE (1952–) American writer and assistant editor of *CoEvolution Quarterly*

HERRING, MARK Y. (1952–) American librarian

HJELMQVIST, BENGT (1903–) Swedish librarian, writer, and developer of Anglo-Scandinavian public library conferences

HODGE, A. A. (1823–1886) American Presbyterian leader

HOLMES, OLIVER WENDELL, SR. (1809–1894) American physician, poet, and essayist

HUBBARD, ELBERT (1856–1915) American writer, publisher, artist, and philosopher

HUGHES, ROBERT (1938–) Australian-born author and art critic

HUGHES, TED (1930–1998) English poet and children's book author

HUGO, VICTOR (1802–1885) French poet, novelist, and statesman

IBN TIBBON, JUDAH (CA. 1150–1230) Jewish philosopher and doctor

JAKES, JOHN (1932–) American fiction writer

JOHNSON, DOUG (1952–) American writer, speaker, and technology/library consultant

JOHNSON, LADY BIRD (1912–2007) American entrepreneur and First Lady of the United States

JOHNSON, SAMUEL (1709–1784) English author

JUDAH HA-LEVI (CA. 1075–1141) Spanish Jewish philosopher and poet

KEILLOR, GARRISON (1942–) American radio personality, storyteller, and humorist

KENNEDY, JOHN F. (1917–1963) Thirty-fifth president of the United States

KEPPEL, FRANCIS (1916–1990) American educator and U.S. Commissioner of Education

KINGSOLVER, BARBARA (1955–) American writer

KIRKPATRICK, ANNA Canadian library patron

KLEIN, NAOMI (1970–) Canadian journalist, author, and activist

KOONTZ, DEAN (1945–) American novelist

KOSINSKI, JERZY (1933–1991) Polish-born American novelist

LAMB, CHARLES (1775–1834) English essayist

L'AMOUR, LOUIS (1908–1988) American western novelist

LEBOWITZ, FRAN (1950–) American author

LONGFELLOW, HENRY WADSWORTH (1807–1882) American poet and educator

LUBBOCK, JOHN (1834–1913) English banker, politician, biologist, and archaeologist

MACLEAN, NORMAN (1902–1990) American author and scholar

MACLEISH, ARCHIBALD (1892–1982) American poet, writer, and Librarian of Congress

MANDELA, NELSON (1918–) President of South Africa and anti-apartheid activist

MANGUEL, ALBERTO (1948–) Argentine-born writer, translator, and editor

MANLEY, WILL (1949–) *American Libraries* columnist and librarian

MÁRQUEZ VILLANUEVA, FRANCISCO (1931–) Spanish-born author and professor of Romance literature

MARTIN, ROBERT S. American librarian, archivist, administrator, and educator

MARX, GROUCHO (1890–1977) American comedian and film star

MCCRACKEN, ELIZABETH (1966–) American author

MEDAWAR, CHARLES English writer and specialist on medical policy and drug safety

MÉLANÇON, ROBERT (1947–) French Canadian author and scholar

MEYER, EDITH PATTERSON (1895–1993) American librarian, editor, and children's book author

MOORE, MICHAEL (1954–) American filmmaker, author, and political commentator

MORRIS, JAN (1926–) British historian, author, and travel writer

MORRISON, TONI (1931–) Nobel Prize–winning American author, editor, and professor

MOYERS, BILL (1934–) American journalist and public commentator

NIGER, SAMUEL (1883–1955) Yiddish literary critic

OBAMA, BARACK (1961–) U.S. senator and forty-fourth president of the United States

OLSEN, ERICA User experience designer for Second Life, and creator of LibrarianAvengers.org

ORTEGA Y GASSET, JOSÉ (1883–1955) Spanish philosopher

ORWELL, GEORGE (1903–1950) English author

OSLER, WILLIAM (1849–1919) Physician, professor, and president of the Bibliographical Society, 1913–1918

PEARL, NANCY (1945–) American librarian, author, and literary critic

PERRY, MICHAEL (1964–) American humorist and author

PLOTNIK, ARTHUR American editor and author

POUNDSTONE, PAULA (1959–) American comedian

POWELL, LAWRENCE CLARK (1906–2001) American librarian, literary critic, and author

PROULX, ANNIE (1935–) American journalist and author

PUTNAM, ROBERT D. (1941–) American political scientist and professor

QUINN, JAMES American librarian

RAYNOR, JOHN P. (1923–1997) American priest and president of Marquette University

RICHARDS, KEITH (1943–) English guitarist, songwriter, and member of the Rolling Stones

RICHTER, JEAN PAUL (1763–1825) German author

ROOSEVELT, ELEANOR (1884–1962) American author, politician, and First Lady of the United States

ROSENBLATT, ROGER American journalist, author, commentator, and professor

ROSZAK, THEODORE (1933–) American scholar and author

ROTH, PHILIP (1933–) American novelist

ROWAN, CARL (1925–2000) American journalist and public servant

RUNDMAN, JONATHAN American singer and songwriter

RUSSELL, WILLY (1947–) British playwright, screenwriter, author, and lyricist

RYAN, PAM MUÑOZ (1951–) American author

SAGAN, CARL (1934–1996) American astronomer, astrochemist, and author

SAWYER, DAVID American columnist and mayor of Sandpoint, Idaho

SAYERS, FRANCES CLARKE (1897–1989) American children's book author, librarian, and educator

SCHAAF, MIV (d.1998) Historical preservationist and *Los Angeles Times* columnist

SCHOPENHAUER, ARTHUR (1788–1860) German philosopher

SCHLESINGER, ARTHUR MEIER, JR. (1917–2007) American historian and social critic

SÉVIGNÉ, MARIE DE (1626–1696) French aristocrat

SHAKESPEARE, WILLIAM (1564–1616) English poet and playwright

SHELDON, SIDNEY (1971–2007) American novelist, playwright, and screenwriter

SHERA, JESSE (1903–1982) American librarian and information scientist

SIZER, THEODORE (1932–) American leader of educational reform

SNICKET, LEMONY (1970–) American author and screenwriter

STOLL, CLIFFORD American astronomer, computer expert, and author

TAYLOR, BAYARD (1825–1878) American poet, translator, and travel writer

TENNANT, ROY American librarian

TETRICK, MEGAN JO American library patron

THOMAS, RICHARD F. (1950–) English-born author and professor of classics

TONA, BEVERLY American journalist

TOTH, SUSAN ALLEN (1940–) American writer

TWAIN, MARK (1835–1910) American humorist, author, and lecturer

VAUGHAN, HENRY (1622–1695) Welsh metaphysical poet and medical practitioner

VEANER, ALLEN B. (1929–) American librarian and author

VONNEGUT, KURT, JR. (1922–2007) American author

WAGNER, JANE (1935–) American producer, director, and Lily Tomlin's comedy writer

WARNER, ROGER English author and director of Squiz.net

WEEKS, LINTON (1951–) American journalist and editor

WEISKEL, TIMOTHY C. American professor, historian, and social anthropologist

WEST, JESSAMYN (1968–) American librarian, blogger, and creator of Librarian.net

WHITE, HERBERT S. (1927–) American writer and professor of library and information science

WIESEL, ELIE (1928–) Jewish writer, professor, political activist, and Nobel Laureate

WINTERSMITH, D. C. SWAN (1839–1912) U.S. postmaster

WOOLF, VIRGINIA (1882–1941) English novelist and essayist

YOUNG, CHARLES E. (1931–) American professor and president of both UCLA and the University of Florida

SOURCES

The gathering of quotes for this book would have been a more difficult process had it not been for the compilation work of others. The following books and websites were very useful in assembling this material:

Brainy Quote—www.brainyquote.com

Collection of Librarian Quotations—www.angelfire.com/tx/StatBook/ libquot1.html

Favorite Library Quotes—http://homepages.gac.edu/~mtwait/favquotes.htm

Goodreads—www.goodreads.com

Imagi-Natives—http://imagi-natives.com

Library Jokes and Funs—www.librarybliss.com

Library, Librarian, and Librarianship Quotes—http://lis.gse.buffalo.edu/ faculty/ellison/quotes/

Quotable Quotes About Libraries—www.ala.org/ala/aboutala/offices/ola/ salquotablequotes.cfm

Quotations About Libraries and Librarians—www.ifla.org/I/humour/ subj.htm

Quote Garden—www.quotegarden.com/libraries.html

Quotes on Reading and Literacy—www.literacyla.org/quotes.htm

Thinkexist—http://thinkexist.com

Valenza, Joyce K.—*Power Tools Recharged.* Chicago: American Library Association—2004.

Wikiquote—http://en.wikiquote.org

As you enter the library, prepare yourself for a grand adventure . . . for inside lies the entire world just waiting to be explored.

TATYANA ECKSTRAND

☞

CATALOGERS ARE SOME OF THE FEW PROFESSIONALS WHO TAKE PRIDE IN BEING ANAL.

TATYANA ECKSTRAND

TATYANA ECKSTRAND is a project manager and senior cataloger at The Donohue Group in Windsor, Connecticut, a contract cataloging firm serving libraries and museums. For twelve years of her career, she supervised technical services departments of academic libraries. She has an MLS from the University of Buffalo and a BA from Kenyon College. Eckstrand contributed to *The Bibliography of Gay and Lesbian Art* (CAA, 1994) and to the University of California–San Diego Library's Reference Guides to Feminist Theory and Gay and Lesbian Studies.

You may also be interested in

The Back Page: Readers can discover everything from the meager to the important in Bill Ott's *The Back Page,* part readers' advisory and part commentary on the world of books and literature, good and not so good. Filled with humor and occasional defiance of the conventional, this book will delight readers with anecdotes, stories, quizzes, and a host of insights into what makes books what they are—those wonderful and magical sources of great thoughts.

The Library: In this remarkable story, Stuart A. P. Murray traces the history of the library from its very beginnings in ancient Babylon and Alexandria to some of the greatest contemporary institutions—the Royal Society of London, the Newberry Library, the Smithsonian Institution, and many others. Nearly two hundred color and black-and-white photos illustrate the fascinating progress of the institution we know today as the library.

The Whole Library Handbook 4: Readers will find fascinating bits of trivia, as well as humorous sections like "How Many Academic Librarians Does It Take to Change a Lightbulb?" and "Advice from Naughty Library Assistants." Also included are thoughtful essays and reprints of important journal articles by noted experts. Full of lists, contacts, resources, and additional references, *The Whole Library Handbook 4* answers all types of library-related questions in a one-stop, must-have guide!

Sacred Stacks: Maxwell's down-to-earth candor combined with scholarly insight is designed to inspire and enlighten her library colleagues. Drawing from history, sociology, and philosophy, *Sacred Stacks* voices the importance of the library profession and libraries as community institutions in a secular time. Librarians, LIS students and educators, and trustees can step into these sacred stacks to reignite meaning in their everyday work.

Check out these and other great titles at www.alastore.ala.org!